"This is a gentle, but quietly challenging book. It looks safe enough; it reads easily; it's short. But it calls with a haunting voice: Is this your God, a judge? Or is this your God, a friend, a supervisor, a mother?

"The author makes us pay attention to the God we have shaped and asks: 'Is this the real God?' He doesn't answer the question. He only asks, respecting God who reveals, and we who receive the revelation."

Dale R. Olen, Ph.D.
Psychologist and Author

"The search for God does not take place up there or out there. All we need do is surface the God who is here, under our nose. This book does that through real and touching stories. After reading it, I began noticing more often the God on my street."

Rev. Frank J. McNulty
Pastor, Roseland, N.J.

"Who is God? This question which seems quite theoretical has very specific consequences. Since we are made to God's image and likeness, who God is (or is conceived) shapes our very identity. Andre Beauchamp invites us to review this central mystery in our lives and adjust our relationship and life-style accordingly."

Robert F. Morneau
Auxiliary Bishop of Green Bay

FOREWORD
Most Rev. Rembert Weakland, O.S.B.
Archbishop of Milwaukee

THE GOD WHO LIVES ON MY STREET

10 VIEWS

ANDRE BEAUCHAMP

TWENTY-THIRD PUBLICATIONS
Mystic, Connecticut 06355

Translated from the French
by Rosemarie Fisher

Illustrations
by William Baker

Twenty-Third Publications
185 Willow Street
P.O. Box 180
Mystic CT 06355
(203) 536-2611
800-321-0411

ISBN 0-89622-506-2
Library of Congress Catalog Card Number 91-67712

FOREWORD

Where do we find God?

Or is that the wrong question?

St. Benedict in his Rule for Monks does not expect the novice to find God (what a relief!). The novice is rather to be evaluated on the search: Does he truly seek God? That is enough.

The seeking is more important than the finding. One finds only glimpses and glimmers anyway.

Our seeking is determined by our inner being. Our world with its ups and downs, bright spots and blinding glares, darkness and uncomfortableness, warmth and chills is where we seek glimpses of God.

Our human relationships help or hinder our search, condition us one way or another. If God is our police officer, then all the authority figures we know and have known point out God to us or hide God from us.

If God is love and we have never been loved nor learned how to love others, we can only seek God in our dream-worlds of waking up beautiful princesses or being awakened by charming princes.

Perhaps we seek God in beauty only to find that most of our world is ugly and depressing.

It is not easy to seek God without models to show us how, without peeping into the lives of others as they, too, seek to go beyond self.

If you do not talk of such things because you are timid or too ashamed, if your vocabulary fails you, then perhaps this book by Andre Beauchamp is just what you need.

Don't forget: What is important is not finding God. Let a glimpse now and again suffice. It is the search for God that counts—and perseverance.

Rembert G. Weakland, O.S.B.
Archbishop of Milwaukee

A wise man was walking beside the sea,
Thinking about God.
"I'm going to know everything about God,"
He thought.
"I'll study God like a clock,
Scrutinizing all the parts.
Then I'll explain to the world
Who God is
Even if I have to write a huge book."
As he walked,
The wise man noticed a child playing on the beach.
The child had dug a large hole in the sand
And was carrying water to it in a small pail—
Once, twice, three times.

"What are you trying to do?" the wise man asked.
"I want to put the entire ocean into this hole,"
The child answered.
"But can't you see that the ocean is much too vast

And the hole much too small?"
The wise man observed.
And the child spoke,
"And you, you think your head can contain God?"

After that day, the wise man gave up his idea.
The mystery of God is limitless.

This small book makes no claim
To say everything about God.
It only hopes to arouse your desire
To know God
And perhaps enable you to know a little more of
Who God is.

God Isn't Always Who We Think
Each person has his or her own idea of God.
In our heads, we form
A certain image of God
Influenced by our life experiences.
What is the value of these images?
What does God say about them,
Since God speaks to us
 In many different ways
In varied and diverse situations
And reveals a little more of the mystery?

What is your favorite image of God?
>   judge
>   father
>   friend
>   boss
>   mother
>   lover
>   wisdom figure

The stories in this book are fictitious,
And yet they are very much like reality.
Everyone should be able to recognize
Himself or herself
In one or more
Of the following characters.
Here is the God who lives on your street.

CONTENTS

M A X

It's when things go bad
That I think about God.

When I'm feeling strong
And everything is going well
I don't think about God.
I don't have time.
I guess God gets along all right without me
Like my elderly mother does
Because I don't have time to see her either.
I'm too busy
With friends, and work,
All sorts of activities,
Meetings,
Or television,
Or simply exhaustion—
In any case, I just don't have the time.

When things go wrong, it seems to me

We're closer to God.
During the last blackout
I was picked up by the police by mistake.
They threw me in jail
Without saying a word,
Without accusing me of anything.
They took my belt
And my shoelaces
To prevent me from doing anything foolish, no doubt.
Believe it or not, that night
I remembered all my prayers.
I was a wreck.
I didn't have to force myself;
I just naturally thought of God.
I felt so small
And I was so afraid
It seemed that all I had to do was raise my eyes
And God understood me.
Underneath it all, it's a lot like my mother.
I don't go to see her often
But when I had that pain in my left arm
And the doctor thought
It might be my heart,
Well, then, I went to see my mother.
I suppose I'd also go see her
To borrow twenty dollars
But I don't think she even keeps that much
In her purse.

I've heard that pimps pray that their business goes well
And that thieves pray that the police won't catch them.
I, well, I prayed to pass my tests
When I was in school.
I prayed to find a job,
I 've prayed to win the lottery,
I pray when I'm sick—
I think about God when things go wrong.
Outside of that, I don't have much time.
It's a little like it is with my mother—
You know how that is.

For Reflection

1. Do I think of God only when things aren't going well?

2. Do I pay attention only to people who have something to give me?

3. Do I consistently ignore those I can help because "I don't have time?"

PAUL

Paul believes in God.
He truly believes,
But he doesn't love God.
He's afraid.
Every time Paul enjoys himself
And has fun
Or takes advantage of life's pleasures
Even without doing anything wrong
He stops and says to himself,
"God's going to punish me.
I know something bad is going to happen."

Sometimes Paul drinks a little too much.
He laughs raucously, sings, plays the clown
And then when he's really tired
He falls asleep, just like that—
All dressed.

In the middle of the night, fear strikes him.

He's afraid to die.
He sees the eye of God
Looking at him,
Condemning him.
"Oh Paul, you're becoming a drunkard
Just like your Uncle Leonard.
Aren't you ashamed of yourself?
You've become an animal,
Your wife is embarrassed,
Your children are ashamed of their father,
You smell of liquor.
Don't you realize that you could die tonight?"
Paul cries out in his sleep,
"No, no, I won't do it again."

Sometimes Paul drinks
To forget his fear
And then he's afraid because he drinks.
He tries to think of God to banish the fear
But in thinking of God
He becomes more fearful.
Paul is running in a circle of fear.

The fear of God
Doesn't lead anywhere.
"Fear of God is the beginning of wisdom"
The proverb says,
But if God only inspires fear

Then you have the wrong address.
Or we might say,
"Try the other side of the street.
God doesn't live here."

For Reflection

1. Does the fear of God overshadow everything I do and think? Why is this so?

2. Am I afraid of God? What is it precisely that I fear about God?
If I am afraid of God, when does this happen most?

3. Do I know anyone like Paul?

4. Can I give any examples of people who try to make others afraid of God?

LUKE

It's a long time since Luke has gone to church.
All of that is just affectation anyway.
Those people are just hypocrites—
They go to church to show off,
They pray together, but don't talk to each other,
Or if they do, it's to gossip about someone else.

When I was young
I went to church to see the girls.
Now guys can see girls at school
Or almost anywhere.
They don't have to go to church for that.

Anyway, I talk to God directly.
I don't need a priest or minister for that
Any more than I need a marriage license
To love my wife.

When I pray

I need to be quiet.
I go out in the country
In the midst of the trees
Near a riverbank
I watch a bird soaring in space
I marvel at the sunset.

And I talk to God—
In my own way, with my own words.
It seems to me that if our world is so beautiful
There must be someone who created it,
A supreme master,
A great spirit.

Nature is my church
It's like an immense temple
Where God is present.
Sitting on the grass, I gaze at everything.
I listen, I smell, I touch
I live in rhythm with nature,
And that's what praying is.

One day I was working in the woods
With my chain saw.
I came to a huge pine
That was to be cut down.
I circled the tree
Looked at it from all angles—

At least 40 inches in diameter at the trunk
And straight as an arrow.
I looked at it again.
It was almost like my grandfather
Looking down at me.
I couldn't do it—
I left with my saw.
It was too beautiful,
I couldn't cut it down.

It seems to me that prayer is like that—
It's finding things so beautiful
That all you can say is thank you.

For Reflection

1. When do I find that I want to pray? In what circumstances? On what occasions?

2. Do I find God in nature?

3. Does having others around prevent me from encountering God?

4. What do I really think of Luke's reason for not going to church?

SYLVIA

I'll never say my prayers again.
I've said too many.

When I was ten years old
And my mother was dying
The doctors bent over her
To watch her life's last breath.
I can still see all the tubes,
The syringes,
The pints of blood that hung beside her bed,
And the busy air of the nurses,
Seeking in vain for a pulse
Under flesh that was already cold.

I still hear the moan that rose
From the body that was already no longer my mother.
At every breath a shudder,
With every shudder a cry,
And every cry an echo from the depths of Earth.

Hail Mary, full of grace.

I prayed, prayed, prayed,
Prayed to the point of being sick,
Prayed enough to have swollen knees,
Prayed till my heart broke,
But in the morning my mother was dead.

Our Father, who art in heaven

I was thirty years old
And my daughter fell off her bike
While crossing the railroad tracks.
The train stopped as fast as it could
But it was too late.
I can still see her on the tracks—
My child,
Who used to scream at the sight of blood,
Lying on the tracks in her own blood.

She was always a joyful child
Who liked to laugh and have fun,
And now I held in my arms
Only a bleeding body.

My daughter, my beautiful little daughter!
And that time I prayed again
From the bottom of my heart
As I never prayed before—
Even more than for my mother,
More even than when my daughter was born,
More than during my own illness.

Holy Mary, Mother of God

I can't pray any more,
Because death comes anyway
To take away mothers and tiny children.
The unbeliever lives for a hundred years
But nothing stops the train
When a little girl
Thoughtlessly crosses the tracks without looking.
There's too much evil in the world,
Too many young girls who are raped
While the abuser leaves the scene laughing,
Too many grocery store owners killed for twenty dollars
While the assassin flees wiping his hands.

I prayed to push away death
But death won.
I prayed with all my heart
But no one heard my cry.
I prayed in vain and now I'll never pray again.

For Reflection

1. What do I usually ask for in prayer?

2. Do I ever pray without asking for something?

3. When I have prayed without being answered, do I revolt against God?

4. How do I judge that my prayer has not been answered?

MARSHA

Marsha is in her twenties.
Like so many others, she doesn't have a steady job
In spite of her diploma and consistent efforts.
She survives by temporary jobs
And unemployment checks
While she waits.
Waits for what, waits for whom?
She doesn't know.

Marsha lives alone
In a small, third-floor apartment
On our street.
There she can live the way she wants,
Listen to music,
Follow her own rhythm.

When Marsha's anxious,
When life is too rough,
When stress overcomes her,
She does yoga and meditates.

She assumes the lotus position,
Breathes deeply, slowly,
Centers her thoughts,
Enters into herself.
In the depths of her body and her spirit
She experiences a new calm and peace.

When she does her yoga,
Marsha doesn't really know what happens to her.
She certainly has a new awareness of her body.
She can escape from the nervous tension
Of the outside world.
It's like an oasis in the desert,
A truce in the middle of a war.
Her body becomes lighter,
Almost escaping the constraints of time and space.
Sometimes Marsha thinks she might be praying—
As though her solitude were inhabited,
As though a Word called to her from inside herself,
As though a personal presence made itself felt.

Sometimes Marsha isn't conscious of anything
Outside herself,
And that doesn't bother her
Because what she's looking for
Isn't contact with something outside
But simply greater self-possession.
She doesn't want to know anything

About anyone else
Not friends, or family, or the world's problems—
Only peace—
To experience peace in her body,
And in her whole being,
To create unity between her body and spirit,
To be at the center of the world,
To be a forgotten island,
Without a shore, lost in the ocean,
To be a star far beyond any constellation.
In that other world she exists, she survives.
In those moments at least, Marsha thinks she is alive.

For Reflection

1. Am I like Marsha?

2. Am I afraid to seek silence and aloneness?

3. Can I be alone with myself in silence and meditate?

4. Is that what I call prayer?

DENNIS

I knew God would punish me.
Didn't my mother always say that when I was young?
"If you do wrong,
God's going to punish you.
God sees everything, you know.
Nothing escapes God,
Even when you hide,
Even when your mother doesn't see you,
Even when no one knows,
God sees you.
God knows everything you do
And writes it all in a big book.
Nothing escapes God
And you have to pay for all your faults."

Maybe my mother said that
Just to scare me.
Sometimes it's easy for parents
To make their children afraid of God
So they can control them.

I was afraid, afraid of everything,
Afraid when I teased my little sister,
Afraid when I cheated in school,
Afraid when I didn't do what my mother said.
I imagined God lying in wait for me in the dark,
Ready to punish me.

When I discovered my homosexuality
I was absolutely terrified.
We can imagine almost anything
But not that.
Sexuality is a problem in itself
With its strong impulses in adolescence
But being homosexual, that seemed so much worse.
You feel everyone's looking at you,
Making fun of you, judging you.
I felt the scorn of everyone around me.
I wanted to hide myself inside the darkest tunnel
To escape the looks, the laughs, the sarcastic remarks,
But above all to escape God's glance
That accused my heart.

One day, I got rid of my fear.
I dared to do what I wanted.
I was absolutely terrified—
But the next day the sun shone as always,
Children still laughed in the street,
The river still ran to the east—
I had been afraid for no reason, I thought.

So I scoffed at God,
I defied everyone.
My delight was to challenge every rule.
I laughed at my mother's fear
And I shouted to the whole world
That God doesn't exist.

Why is it that fear has now re-entered my life?
My body languishes with exhaustion,
My hair is falling out and my strength is gone.
The doctor spoke the dreaded word, AIDS
I can hear people laughing, enjoying their revenge:
"He's being punished for the way he sinned.
It is God's vengeance."
Did God take stock of my deeds
And deliver me to this death?
I don't think so.
But I look to my brothers and sisters
For a little concern, a sign of tenderness,
A simple smile that would rekindle hope.

For Reflection

1. Do I associate God with fear and with always watching me to catch me? Why?

2. Do I try to establish contact with people who have been rejected from various groups? Am I insensitive to their needs?

3. What role, if any, does fear of God have in my life?

JANICE

Janice is forty.
In pain and misery
She raised four children
On the south side of Chicago,
Amid cold, humidity, hunger
Always trying to get by,
Supporting an alcoholic husband,
Struggling to live in spite of it all,
And never daring to hope for anything better.

It isn't that bad.
We always manage somehow.
There are people worse off than we are.
We were born to have little
And we're lucky to have what we do.

Frank, Janice's oldest,
Left home too soon
With the dream of making easy money,
Living the high life.
He started selling drugs

Got caught in a raid—
Six years in prison.

Lorraine, her daughter,
Also wanted an easy life.
She's a pretty girl and knows how to please men.
She gets along.
With an apartment downtown
She's living in the fast lane.
She had a child six years ago
And couldn't take care of him—
So Janice is raising him.

Peter and Linda, the two youngest,
Have also left home to start their own lives.
Peter works in construction
And has a job in Colorado now.
Linda's been living with her boyfriend for two years
And they're thinking of getting married soon.
Janice bears her life with patience.
It's not all that bad, as she sees it,
And since her husband left,
At least there's peace.

Young people want to change everything
Even if they get hurt.
They're too ambitious.
There have always been the poor and the rich—

God wants it that way—
There are mice and there are cats,
Then there are dogs that chase the cats,
And even big dogs that bite smaller dogs.

Nothing is perfect
And we have to learn to be content
With what we have.
There will always be people who are poor.
When you're poor, it's because God loves you.

God tests those who are most beloved
Even if it sometimes hurts.
It's a shame my children never understood that.
Maybe I wasn't a good mother for them—
Or if my husband had only been supportive.
But we have to admit that we who are poor
Aren't made for happiness.
At least God is still there for us
Asking only that we do our duty.

For Reflection

1. Am I like Janice?

2. Do I think poverty is a sign of God's love?

3. Do I try to improve my life?

4. Does God really ask passive submission from us?

5. How did Jesus relate to the poor?

TOM

Suddenly that day Tom needed
The address of his Uncle Roger
Who was now living in Orlando, Florida.
The last time he came to Minnesota
Uncle Roger had told Tom
"Why don't you come and spend your vacation with us?
Here's my address.
I'm only giving it to you, though—
I don't want to see the others.
You're my favorite nephew and you're okay.
You remind me of my son—killed in Vietnam.
When you feel like coming
Give me a call or write
And come on down."
Tom had put the paper safely away.
Who knows? Someday it might be useful.
Two years later he decided to go see Uncle Roger.
But first of all he had to find the address.
He searched high and low for that paper.

He emptied the top drawer
Stuffed with telephone and electric bills,
The children's pictures,
And various important papers,
But he never found Uncle Roger's address.

By the second day
Tom had looked through everything—
Envelopes, photo albums,
Magazines, books,
Waste baskets,
The children's toys,
The glove compartment in the car,
Even on top of the refrigerator.

The next day
He made a promise to St. Anthony
Patron of desperate cases of lost articles.
When he was young and had lost
A ball or any object
He would throw his rosary in the air
And the direction the cross was pointing to
When it fell to earth
Would guide him to what he was looking for.
Or he would pray to St. Anthony:
"Holy St. Anthony,
Patron of desperate causes,
Patron of lost articles,

Help me find my ball
And I'll say three Hail Marys."

Maybe St. Anthony
Could really help him now.
Remembering his former debts
He said two decades of the rosary
Because he had frequently forgotten
Some of those three Hail Marys.
Then he prayed from the bottom of his heart
"Holy St. Anthony
Help me find my Uncle Roger's address
And I promise I'll donate twenty dollars
To charity in thanksgiving."
Convinced he would find it
He began his search again.
Friday, Saturday, Sunday—
It was no use.

Then anger overtook him.
Moody, frustrated,
He got in his car to calm down.
At the first stop sign he simply slowed down,
Turned without signaling,
Then rapidly accelerated.
On raising his eyes to the rear-view mirror
He saw the flashers on the police car.
Why does misfortune always come

In twos or threes?
"You're in a hurry, my friend?
No stop, no signals, speeding—
Can I see your driver's license?"
Tom kept telling himself
"I mustn't get angry
Keep control of yourself, smile, be polite.
Stay cool, Tom.
It's nothing, nothing,
It'll be over soon."
He fumbled through his wallet,
Pulled out his papers, driver's license,
Registration,
Then underneath, the insurance certificate.
And there folded in four,
Uncle Roger's address!
He let out a curse in frustration
And then a deep sigh of relief.

The next day
Tom drove to Winona
On the banks of the Mississippi River.
He took a rock
Wrapped a twenty dollar bill around it
And held it in place with two elastic bands.
He stepped back a few paces
And threw the stone with all his strength
Into the river below.

"There, St. Anthony,
I'm bringing you that twenty dollars.
I looked so hard for that paper
Now you look for the twenty dollars—
It's your turn."

For Reflection

1. Am I like Tom, making deals with God or a saint?

2. If I bargain with God, why do I usually do it?

3. Do I demand that God do what I want?

PAULINE

I have to tell you—
I have discovered God.

At first, I was a regular churchgoer.
Religion was part of my life
Very naturally.
It was like breathing, eating, or working—
It had to be part of my life.
I was a fairly submissive woman
Who listened to the priest
Just as I listened to my husband.

Then one day everything shattered,
My husband left me for another woman—
Me and the children.
I learned what misery really is.
I understood how many of us women
Are dominated by men
Whether it's our father,

Our husband,
The priest, the mayor, a boss,
Or even our own sons.

We tell our daughters to be quiet
And yield to the boys.
Boys do what they want,
But we don't let anything get by with the girls.
One day, I had enough
Of obedience, of submission,
Of a social structure built against us.

It took me ten years of struggle,
Of courage,
To learn to live independently.
First of all to survive
And then to live,
To organize myself,
To feel good about myself.
I was angry
And my revolt isn't over yet.

The religion of my childhood
Dissolved with my childishness.
I hate submission,
I detest imposed expectations
Because this is violence
Done to us, to women.

It was through that struggle that I discovered God.
First of all, I discovered that my fight
Wasn't only my fight
But that of all women—
A fight to gain an equal chance,
A decent salary,
Day-care centers, health services, information,
Needed resources to change our lives.
I discovered the struggles of our neighborhood—
Those of battered women,
Those of the unemployed,
Those of men and women
Whose lives have been ravaged by alcohol.

I discovered beautiful people
Who struggle to overcome all this,
Who have learned to hope,
And who don't wait for their death
To begin to live.

It's there that I discovered true believers:
Young people, the elderly,
Some with education, others without—
But all those who say God doesn't accept injustice,
That God sends the rich away empty
And fills the hungry with good things.

Through contact with them, I discovered Jesus.

Blessed are those who hunger and thirst for justice.
Jesus empowers us to go beyond ourselves,
He leads us to full liberation.

We gather to pray,
To sing,
To reflect on Jesus' life
And on our own,
On his actions and ours
In order to discover our way of being faithful today.

"Love one another."
It's hard to live that rule,
To take it really seriously,
But I think I'm beginning to learn how.

I'm a fighter
And I want to keep on being a fighter
Now that I've discovered faith in Jesus.

It seems to me that I'm happier than before,
Freer,
More patient.
I hope it's only a beginning
Because I want to continue the struggle.

For Reflection

1. Am I like Pauline?

2. Do I see unjust situations around me? What are they?

3. Do I commit myself to changing these situations?

4. "Think globally; act locally." What can I do in regard to each of these?

5. Are the justice struggles I'm committed to a road to faith?

STEPHEN

I used to think God must really be boring.
I remember
When I was a little boy
I had to be quiet
And sit up very straight at the end of the bench,
Or kneel
With my nose in the back of the person
 In front of me
While my mother whispered,
"Look at God."
I looked all around—
I didn't see anything.
There were the huge columns,
The sanctuary, the communion rail, the pulpit
The altar, the candles,
The large Bible—
But I didn't see God.

My mother closed her eyes,
Her lips moved in silence.
I kept searching obstinately.

Where is God?
My mother found God with her eyes closed.
I looked and couldn't see anything.
I searched without finding,
She found without searching.
And when we'd leave church
She'd say,
"You see, it's good
To visit with God."

Me, I thought it was great
To finally be outside on the street,
And I thought to myself that God
Would really be happier
To stay outdoors
In the midst of the world
Instead of staying cooped up in a church.
That was my life's big discovery—
God lives outside
In the streets, in the midst of the people,
Where there's weeping, singing, screaming, dancing
Where there's laughter.

I know that God
Isn't boring.
I'll tell you more about it in a little while
Because now my mother says I'm bothering her
And keeping her from praying.

For Reflection

1. Do I have childhood memories about God? What are they?

2. Are these memories connected to my father, my mother, or someone else?

3. Is God only to be found in a holy place, or in the midst of the world and people?

GETTING RID OF GOD
In Order to Find God

Many people talk about God
And say that
God is this, God is that,
And say just about anything about God—
Or almost.
They may keep us in fear,
Or in fatalism,
Or in subjection,
Without ever leading us to love, to joy.

For our part, because of our Christian faith,
We look to Jesus as our primary guide to God.
He tells us his Father's secrets,
He gives us a taste for living,
Living now and eternally.
In a way, we have to rid ourselves of God
To find God,
Rid ourselves of the God we have invented
To discover the God who speaks a name
And shows us a face
In Jesus Christ, our brother, our friend, our savior.

Let's rid ourselves of the God of blind fate
Who has made things the way they are

Forever and always,
The God who takes pleasure in human suffering,
Who allows children to die and mothers to weep,
Who made the rich and the poor alike,
And who said to the poor
"Put up with your misery."
Let's rather believe in the God of Jesus Christ
Who joins us in the commitment
To change how things are,
Who enters human life,
Who is born, who suffers, who dies
To save the world,
To free us,
Who gives us a taste for life
And who makes us responsible for our lives
Personally and collectively.

Let's rid ourselves of the God of fear
Who criticizes, judges, condemns,
Who watches our every action,
Preserving them forever in a great book,
Who never forgets anything—
Especially the wrong we do—
The God who is vengeful, restraining, malicious,
The sadistic God who keeps repeating
The same negative pronouncements.
Let's believe in the God of Jesus Christ
Who welcomes sinners

And loves to forgive
For we only rescue what we love.
God so loved the world
That God gave an only Son
To show that love
Because God is love.
The person who doesn't love isn't really alive.

And let's rid ourselves of the distant God
Who looks down on us from above
And who isn't really part of our lives,
The God of ideas,
The God of abstraction,
Who has no face, no desires, no hands,
Who is always somewhere else,
Lost in the great beyond
And who drifts, totally unaffected
Like a cloud above our world.
But let's believe in the God of Jesus Christ,
Man among humankind,
Who sings, laughs, and cries,
Who takes pleasure in music
And is deeply moved by a flower in bloom,
A God who is close, one of us, committed to us,
A God who walks with us,
And who in that journey
Leads us beyond the path we would have taken
To other shores, to other lands.

Let's rid ourselves of the God of my little world—
My own little God—
Who comforts me when I hurt
And who forgets everyone else,
A "cautious" God
Who is ready to bear
My scrapes, my hurts, my joys,
And who keeps me safe
From other men and women.
Let's believe in the God of Jesus Christ
Who comes to save a people
Who gathers sisters and brothers into unity,
Who calls all humanity
From the four corners of Earth,
Who breaks down all barriers,
Who loves the yellow, the white, the black
And wants to make them all members of one body,
As the grains of wheat
From many fields
Become one flour and one bread.
Just as the men and women
Drawn together by Jesus
Become one body,
One people filled with hope.

Let's rid ourselves of the God of suffering,
The one who makes people suffer

Because "God loves them"
And the greater that love, the greater the suffering,
The God who tests people—
Without stopping, without mercy—
Even the best among us.
Let's believe in the God of Jesus
Who doesn't like suffering
And who fights against it with us
In every recess of our being,
But who, when suffering is inevitable,
Becomes our companion in distress
And suffers with us
Until our Easter morning.

Let's rid ourselves of the God of might
Who is all-powerful
Who foresees everything ahead of time
And who uses men and women
Simply as puppets
To manipulate.
Let's believe in the God of Jesus Christ
Who is the God of weakness,
A God who surrenders power
Because it only leads to injustice and violence,
A God who became humble and small,
Poor among the poor,
And who, renouncing the prestige of royalty,
Became obedient

Even to death, even to the cross,
The God whose hands are tied,
Who has no weapons, no money,
Who will not choose violence,
Who only has the power of love,
But who, because of that,
Shattered our world.

Let's rid ourselves of the God of the cosmic forces
Who would be energy
Or wind, or sun,
The God of the thunderbolts
Or of beautiful summer days,
The God of nature,
The God of the great cosmos
Where everything mingles together,
Plants, animals, migrating spirits,
Lost in the thoughtlessness of matter.
Let's believe in the God of Jesus Christ
Who is above all Someone,
Who is Mother, Father, Friend
And who enters into dialogue
With men and women,
Who gives them the Word,
Who speaks to their ears and to their hearts
So that love
Can exist between God and them.

We will never totally know who God is.
No one has seen God
Except the Son
And those to whom the Son has revealed God.
Jesus leads us to his Father.
He shows us God's face,
Enlivens us with God's breath, the Spirit.
When we move closer to the God of Jesus Christ
We discover the secret of God,
Loving Parent, Son, and Spirit—
And it is then that we really begin to live.